THE ARK BUILDER'S HELPERS

5 Bedtime Stories of the Small Creatures of the Flood

BLUME POTTER

INTRODUCTION

Imagine sharing a story with your child or grandchild that not only brings the Bible to life but also teaches the timeless values of courage, teamwork, and faith. The Ark Builder's Helpers: 5 Bedtime Stories of the Small Creatures of the Flood is more than just a collection of bedtime tales—it's a journey through one of the most beloved stories from the Bible, told through the eyes of the smallest and often overlooked creatures.

These beautifully crafted stories are designed to captivate young minds while reinforcing important life lessons. Each chapter highlights the incredible contributions of God's smallest creations—ants, spiders, songbirds, mice, and fireflies—showing how even the tiniest among us have a special role to play in God's plan.

As you tuck your little ones in at night, let these stories be a source of comfort and inspiration. They'll learn that no matter their size, they have the power to make a big difference in the world. Filled with warmth, faith, and the gentle lessons of the Bible, this book is a must-have for every family's bedtime routine.

Let The Ark Builder's Helpers light the way for your child's imagination and heart, guiding them to sleep with the knowledge that God's love and plan includes everyone—no matter how small.

CHAPTER ONE:
THE ANTS' ARMY

In the days before the great flood, as Noah and his family began the enormous task of building the Ark, the world buzzed with activity. But while the towering trees were felled by strong hands, and the mighty animals began to prepare for the journey, a much smaller, yet equally important task force was quietly at work.

Deep in the ground, beneath the roots of an old oak tree, lived a colony of ants. These ants were known for their hard work and their strong sense of duty. They might have been small, but they knew they had an important role to play in the grand plan that God had set into motion.

The Ant Queen, wise and thoughtful, called a meeting with her colony. "My dear ants," she began, "we have received a special task. Noah, the Ark builder, needs our help. Though we are small, our efforts can make a big difference. We will gather the tiny pieces that others might overlook—the leaves, the twigs, the seeds. Each of us will carry what we can, and together, we will contribute to the building of the Ark."

The ants nodded in agreement, their antennae twitching with determination. They knew this was a job for all of them, from the youngest worker to the oldest forager. There was no time to waste, and no contribution was too small.

And so, the ants set to work. They marched in long, orderly lines, each ant carrying a bit of straw, a fragment of leaf, or a speck of soil. They worked tirelessly, from dawn until dusk, never stopping, never complaining. Their tiny legs moved quickly, and their small bodies carried loads many times their size.

As the days passed, Noah noticed the piles of gathered materials growing larger. He saw the ants at work and marveled at their dedication. "Even the smallest of God's creatures have a role to play in His plan," Noah thought, smiling to himself.

The ants continued their work, day after day, never faltering. They knew that the Ark would not be complete without their contributions, and they took pride in their efforts. Through their diligence and teamwork, the ants showed that even the tiniest creatures can have a mighty impact when they work together.

By the time the Ark was ready to set sail, the ants had done their part. The small twigs and leaves they had gathered were woven into the structure, helping to strengthen the great vessel. As the rain began to fall, the ants retreated to their underground home, knowing they had fulfilled their duty.

And so, the story of the Ants' Army became a lesson for all—the lesson that no matter how small you are, your contribution matters. Every effort, every bit of work, counts in God's grand design. The ants had proven that

even the smallest creatures could play a big role in
building something great.

CHAPTER TWO:
THE SPIDERS' WEBS

As the Ark took shape, towering over the landscape, there was much more to be done. Noah and his family worked tirelessly, but they weren't alone in their efforts. High in the trees and hidden in the corners of the great wooden structure, a group of spiders watched with keen eyes. They saw the beams being raised, the planks being fastened, and the Ark slowly coming together.

The Spider Leader, an old and wise orb-weaver, gathered her fellow spiders for a meeting. "We have a special gift," she began, her voice soft but firm. "Our webs are strong and flexible, perfect for securing the delicate parts of the Ark. The winds will blow, and the rain will pour, but with our help, the Ark will hold steady. Let us use our skills to assist in this great task."

The spiders agreed, eager to play their part. They were proud of their ability to spin intricate webs, and they knew that their contribution would make a difference. They scurried across the beams and planks, finding the perfect spots to weave their webs. Each thread was placed with care, each web spun with precision.

The spiders worked together, their webs connecting the beams, reinforcing the joints, and securing loose ends. Their webs were nearly invisible, yet incredibly strong, holding everything in place. As they worked, they felt a sense of purpose and pride. They weren't just spinning webs; they were helping to protect the Ark, ensuring that it would stay strong during the coming storm.

Noah noticed the spiders' work as he inspected the Ark. He gently touched one of the webs and marveled at its strength. "These spiders have truly been a blessing," he thought. "Their delicate webs will help keep everything secure, just as God intended."

As the days passed, the spiders continued their work, weaving and reinforcing the Ark until it was ready for the flood. They knew that their contribution, though small and unseen, was vital. The storm would test the strength of the Ark, but the spiders had faith in their webs.

When the rain finally began to fall, the Ark creaked and groaned as it was lifted by the rising waters. But thanks to the spiders' webs, everything stayed in place. The Ark held firm, and the animals inside were safe. The spiders, nestled in their corners, felt a deep sense of satisfaction. They had used their unique gifts to serve a greater purpose.

And so, the story of the Spiders' Webs became a reminder that everyone has something special to offer. The spiders had shown that their delicate, intricate work was just as important as the heavy lifting done by others. By using their gifts, they had contributed to something far greater than themselves, proving that no talent is too small when it comes to fulfilling God's plan.

CHAPTER THREE:
THE SONGBIRD SCOUTS

As the Ark neared completion, Noah knew it was time to gather the animals. But how would they all find their way to the Ark? The task seemed overwhelming, but help came from above—in the form of a flock of songbirds.

These songbirds were known far and wide for their beautiful melodies. Every morning, their songs filled the air, bringing joy to all who heard them. But on this special occasion, the songbirds had a new mission. The Songbird Leader, a bright and cheerful lark, called the flock together.

"My fellow songbirds," the lark began, her voice clear and melodious, "God has given us a special task. We are to guide the animals to the Ark with our songs. Our melodies will lead them to safety, where they will be protected from the coming flood. We are the heralds of God's plan, and our voices will show the way."

The songbirds fluttered their wings in excitement. They were thrilled to play such an important role. Without delay, they took to the skies, spreading out in all directions. As they flew, they sang their most enchanting songs, melodies that carried far and wide over the land.

The animals heard the sweet, uplifting tunes and followed the sound. The birds' songs led them through forests and fields, over hills and rivers, until they reached the Ark.

The lions, elephants, deer, and even the tiniest creatures marched toward the great vessel, drawn by the songbirds' beautiful music.

Noah watched as the animals arrived, two by two, and he smiled with gratitude. "These songbirds have truly been a blessing," he thought. "Their songs have guided the animals to safety, just as God intended."

The songbirds continued to sing until every animal was aboard the Ark. Their hearts swelled with joy, knowing they had led others to a place of refuge. They perched on the branches near the Ark, their voices still echoing in the air, a symbol of hope and guidance.

When the rain began to fall, the songbirds huddled together, satisfied with their work. They knew they had fulfilled their purpose, using their songs to lead others to safety. The Songbird Leader chirped softly to the flock, "We have shown that guidance and leadership can come in many forms. Today, we used our voices to bring others to a place of refuge. We have done our part in God's plan."

And so, the story of the Songbird Scouts became a lesson in guidance and leadership. The songbirds had proven that leading others to safety is a joyful and noble task. Their melodies, once just a source of beauty, had become a beacon of hope, showing that even the smallest creatures can be leaders when they use their gifts for the greater good.

CHAPTER FOUR:
THE MICE'S MISSION

As the Ark stood ready, with animals arriving from every corner of the earth, there was one more critical task to be completed. Deep in the grass near the Ark, a small family of mice lived quietly, always careful to stay out of sight. They were tiny and timid, often scurrying away at the first sign of danger. But on this day, they had a mission that required courage.

The Mouse Leader, a wise and cautious elder, gathered his family together. "We have been given an important task," he began, his voice soft but determined. "God has entrusted us with gathering seeds and grains to store on the Ark. These will be the food that will keep everyone alive during the flood. Though we are small and the larger animals may frighten us, our work is vital for the survival of all on board."

The young mice looked at each other nervously. The thought of venturing near the big animals filled them with fear, but they also understood the importance of their mission. They knew they couldn't let their fears stop them from doing what was needed.

With a deep breath, the mice set out on their task. They scurried through the fields, gathering seeds and grains in their tiny paws. They moved quickly, working together to collect as much as they could. Whenever they saw a large animal, they would pause, their little hearts pounding, but then they would remind themselves of their mission and continue on.

As they worked, they discovered something surprising. The larger animals, though imposing, were too busy with their own tasks to notice the small mice. The mice realized that their fears were unfounded, and this gave them the confidence to complete their mission.

By the time the rain clouds gathered in the sky, the mice had stored away plenty of seeds and grains on the Ark. They had braved their fears and accomplished something crucial for the survival of everyone on board. The Mouse Leader looked at the piles of food and nodded with pride. "We may be small, but we have shown great courage. Our work will help sustain life during the flood."

Noah noticed the mice's efforts and was filled with gratitude. "These tiny creatures have done something truly important," he thought. "They have gathered the food that will keep us all alive. Their bravery in the face of fear is a testament to the power of even the smallest among us."

As the rain began to fall, the mice huddled together in their cozy nook on the Ark, safe and warm. They had faced their fears and completed their mission, proving that even the smallest tasks are essential when it comes to God's plan.

And so, the story of the Mice's Mission became a lesson in courage and the importance of every contribution. The mice had shown that overcoming fear and completing even

the smallest tasks can have a big impact. Their bravery
and dedication were a reminder that everyone, no matter
how small, has an essential role to play.

CHAPTER FIVE:
THE FIREFLY'S LIGHT

As the rain poured down and the Ark swayed gently on the rising waters, darkness filled the sky. Inside the Ark, the animals huddled together, safe but frightened. The storm outside was fierce, and the night seemed endless. It was in this moment of fear and uncertainty that a tiny, flickering light appeared.

High in the corners of the Ark, a group of fireflies had taken refuge. They were small, delicate creatures, but they had a special gift—one that was desperately needed during this dark time. The Firefly Leader, an older, wise firefly, gathered the others together.

"My fellow fireflies," he began, his tiny light glowing softly, "the storm outside is strong, and the night is dark. But we have been given a special gift, the gift of light. Let us use our light to bring comfort and hope to those around us. We may be small, but our light can make a big difference."

The fireflies nodded in agreement. They knew their light could help ease the fears of the animals in the Ark. With a flutter of wings, they spread out, each firefly finding a spot where their light would shine the brightest.

As the fireflies began to glow, a warm, gentle light filled the Ark. The animals, who had been restless and afraid, began to calm down. The soft, golden glow of the fireflies brought a sense of peace and comfort. The darkness was still there, but it didn't seem so overwhelming with the fireflies' light guiding the way.

The fireflies felt a deep sense of honor as they lit up the Ark. They knew their light was helping to bring hope in a time of fear. As they floated above the animals, their lights twinkling like stars, they realized that even in the darkest times, there was always a way to bring comfort and hope.

Noah noticed the fireflies' light and was deeply moved. "These small creatures have brought light into the darkness," he thought. "Their gentle glow has calmed the storm within, just as God's light brings peace to troubled hearts."

As the storm continued outside, the fireflies kept their lights shining, never wavering. They knew their task was important, and they were proud to fulfill it. The animals, comforted by the light, settled down to sleep, knowing they were safe.

And so, the story of the Firefly's Light became a lesson in hope and comfort. The fireflies had shown that even in the darkest of times, a little light can make a big difference. Their bravery and dedication reminded everyone on the Ark that, no matter how small, each of us has the power to bring light and hope to others.